Marriage Wisdom

FOR HER

Marriage Wisdom

FOR HER

A 31 DAY DEVOTIONAL
FOR BUILDING A BETTER MARRIAGE

MATTHEW AND LISA JACOBSON

LOYAL
ARTS MEDIA

© 2017 by Matthew L. Jacobson and Lisa Jacobson

Published by
Loyal Arts Media
P.O. Box 1414
Bend, OR 97709
loyalartsmedia.com

Printed in the United States of America

Cover painting by Lance Austin Olsen
Cover design by Jamie Drouin

ISBN 978-1-929125-55-5 (paperback)

Table of Contents

Introduction

"She opens her mouth with wisdom; and on her tongue is the law of kindness."
(Proverbs 31:26)

Wisdom.

Who would have thought that such small truths could bring about such big changes?

But they can.

And they do.

And it's why growing in wisdom is a real marriage-changer.

It's a marriage-changer because once we see the direct connection between the things that we say and do . . . and the kind of relationship we want to have . . . then we are truly in a place to make a powerful impact on our marriage.

Some people call the insights that Matthew and I are sharing here with you "secrets" – the mysterious keys to a successful marriage. And people ask us for this kind of advice all the time. They want to know the secret to a close and loving relationship.

But what if it isn't really a secret? What if a strong marriage is simply based on biblical principles instead? What if it's based on learning relational truths that are not really a secret at all?

So, no more secrets. Matthew and I have set out to share the insights and wisdom that we've gathered over our own 24 years of marriage together. We're letting you in on those things that work well in marriage, as well as the things that do not. Here you'll find some steps to take and others to avoid. You'll find encouragement, as well as practical application of Biblical truths in marriage.

You'll also find that we take turns. I share something and then Matthew goes next and so on. This way you're getting to hear from the two of us – from a wife's perspective and from a husband's – and benefit from both.

You'll see that each chapter begins with a short bit of wisdom and then ends with a prayer and small "assignment." Take the time to go through each one. Ask God to show you how you can apply these principles to your own marriage.

Then get ready to walk in wisdom and grow in love.

And watch God change your marriage.

MATT AND LISA

1

A Great Marriage

by Lisa

*Great marriages go the distance
because two people put distance
between themselves and selfishness.*

I can't tell you the exact time or place that I made the decision. But I knew – from the bottom of my heart – that I wanted a great marriage from a surprisingly young age.

Not great as in "grand" but great as in *good*. Strong, close, and even sweet; great as in long-lasting.

But it's one thing to decide it. And another to live it.

And it wasn't too long into our marriage that I realized there was something standing in the way of our having that great marriage that I was so eager to enjoy. We both sensed an invisible barrier keeping us from achieving an incredible relationship. Invisible, but powerful all the same.

That barrier was selfishness.

His selfishness, for sure.

But mine too.

Ouch. I think recognizing my own selfishness in our relationship was ten times harder than seeing his. His self-centeredness was so obvious – the numerous ways he could put his own wants and needs before mine.

But me? I feel like I'm a giver, pouring myself out constantly in a hundred different ways.

I cook, clean up after, and care for him, and the rest of my family too. I get up early and stay up late. And I'm always there for him.

I don't think that sounds very selfish ... do you?

Except for one thing – some selfishness is less apparent than others. And I happen to be an expert in subtle selfishness.

Maybe you are too.

Yes, perhaps we give, but is there a "price tag" that comes with that giving? We pour out ... but not necessarily freely. Maybe even bitterly or greedily. We want – even demand – certain things in return. But if giving comes with a price, then it isn't really giving, is it? And it's not a place in which a loving marriage can thrive.

Okay, but what about my husband? So what about him and his selfishness? It hardly seems fair that the wife should do all the giving. Don't we deserve more than that?

The world has an answer for you. They'll tell you that what you should do is look out for yourself more. That you should outpace him when it comes to the game of selfishness.

But the Bible has a different answer, and it's going to sound counter-intuitive. "Take up your cross daily and follow me." (Luke 9:23)

You will only find your life by focusing on living for Jesus – the One Who gave, and gave, and gave, and keeps giving His life for you, in spite of your disregard for Him.

It's time to pause and to consider Him.

His love for you, His forgiveness for you, His compassion for you . . . .

Turning your heart to Jesus is the best way to find yourself and it's the best hope for your marriage. It gives you the power to take down the walls that have built up between you and your husband, to speak the truth in love, and to offer a kind act in return for a selfish one.

Dear Lord,

I do feel like I give a lot, but I know I am prone to selfishness. I pray You will remind me when those selfish impulses arise — especially when I'm making my husband feel as if I'm choosing for me and not for us. I know You are not asking me to ignore my needs but to be on guard against my natural inclinations to look after myself first. I desire to grow and mature in this. Help me to be selfless, just as You called me to walk.

In Jesus' name, amen.

ASK YOUR HUSBAND:

"What are some ways that I show selfishness in our marriage? Do you ever feel like you 'pay a price' for what I offer to you?"

Notes

Notes

2

The Discreet Wife

by Matthew

*The discreet wife soon discovers
her influence with her husband soars,
because his heart can trust her.*

He may be a quiet accountant, a bold firefighter, an expert plumber, a smart lawyer, a good doctor, a successful salesman, or any number of other professions, but there is one need that transcends all of his character traits and career choices:

He needs to be able to trust you with all of his heart.

He won't use those words, but that's his root concern. Does he know, beyond any doubt, that you are completely trustworthy? Is he confident that, regardless of who you may be talking to, you will never betray his trust, divulge information he feels is sensitive, or reveal anything he would want to be kept between you and him?

(Of course, this is *not* to be understood as ever suggesting that sin should be covered up.)

Are you a woman of discretion?

You have close female friends, and there are extended family relationships that are also close. You want to be open and transparent with them, don't you? You can be, but the woman of discretion never crosses the line when it comes to her husband's privacy and other matters he doesn't want to be discussed outside of his "inner circle," which is you and him.

Be ready for challenge. There will be people in your life who will try to break down the wall of loyalty you have for your husband, feeling that because of the long-standing relationship you've had with them, it's their right to be let in on every detail.

Don't let others dictate where that line of separation is. Let loyalty and faithfulness to your marriage and to your husband's wishes establish the line.

Regarding the trustworthy wife, the Bible puts it like this, "His heart safely trusts in her." (Proverbs 31:11)

Are you a safe place for him? There's no safety without trust, and without trust, there can be no true loyalty. Life is a field of battle for a man. Regardless of his profession, he can only move forward with confidence if he never has to question that you "have his back."

When your husband knows he is married to his most trusted confidant, your influence soars.

If you've not been discreet in the past, then you've damaged that trust. But take heart, it can be restored. Go to your husband and ask him to forgive you, telling him he will never have to worry – ever – again.

If you've walked as a woman of discretion, your husband already trusts you but will still enjoy hearing you tell him that you are loyal and behind him 100%.

Every husband wants to be able to trust his wife implicitly. It's in your power to ensure that his heart can safely trust in you.

Dear Lord,

I pray that I increasingly become a mature, discreet woman. I pray that my husband feels a sense of security and complete trust in me. Help me to guard those things that he wants to be kept private and between only us. Help me always to be his trusted confidant, and prompt me by Your Holy Spirit if I ever begin to speak in a manner that would compromise his trust in me.

In Jesus' name, amen.

Ask your husband:

"Do you feel you can trust me to keep our private things private? Have I ever done something that made you feel insecure or that made you feel it was risky to take me into your confidence? Please know that I intend to be your discreet, completely trustworthy wife."

Notes

Notes

3
The Encourager
by Lisa

She who lifts up her husband when he is down
will find she has a friend for life.

I couldn't say when I first noticed.

We were in the middle of so many trials that it's hard to tell when it actually began. Troubles in the church. Hardships at home. Challenges at work. So much was swirling about us that I didn't notice how heavy it was on his soul.

But then one day I watched as he walked by with his shoulders slumped over and his stride too slow. As if burdened by some great weight and it was all he could do to carry it across the floor.

My heart went out to him. I was rather worried and a little afraid. I mean, what do you do when your man is down? Discouraged? Defeated?

Maybe your husband is different than mine. But mine doesn't necessarily want me to come in and deliver a powerful sermon, or even a spiritual *rah-rah*. He doesn't appreciate me stating the obvious or reminding him of one more way he's failed.

Let's face it, pointing out to him – "It doesn't seem like you're walking in the Spirit, dear." – isn't all that helpful. So what can a wife do to encourage her husband when he's spiritually down?

You can call out to God on his behalf. And this doesn't mean an ordinary "pray for him." This is about true supplication; a crying out to God to work in his life. To minister, convict, or encourage him – depending on the need.

And you don't need to nag or badger him. If anything, this approach only makes things worse.

Put your energies towards those things that will help.

Notice the good things he does.

Be grateful for the little things, such as saying grace around the table or sitting next to each other at church. Appreciate any kind word or thoughtful gesture he might make. Keep in mind that when a person is down, he is often down on himself most of all. So point out the good you can see that he might not realize.

And get rid of any spiritual list you might have made.

You know, the things you think he *should* or *shouldn't* do to be spiritual. No one wants to live up to someone else's personal list of what qualifies as "spiritual." If it's not spelled out in the Bible? Then ditch it. If it is? Then let the Holy Spirit do His job (not you).

Last of all, don't underestimate the power of your own testimony. You can have a tremendous impact on your husband by quietly shining the love of Christ in your home. A soft smile, a gentle word, and a song in your heart can have a stronger influence than might be immediately apparent.

So shine on, sister.

He'll be encouraged.

"Anxiety in the heart of man causes depression, but a good word makes it glad." (Proverbs 12:25)

Dear Lord,

I pray that You will show me how I can encourage my husband when he's feeling discouraged. Help me to be a positive influence in his life and keep me from having a condemning spirit toward him. Give me eyes to see all the ways that I can lift him up when he's feeling down.

In Jesus' name, amen.

ASK YOUR HUSBAND:

"What are some things I can do to help you when you're having a hard time in your soul? Are there certain things I can do (or not do), say (or not say) that would bless and encourage you?"

Notes

Notes

4

A Forgiving Heart

by Matthew

She who finds the key to unlock the prison door
and she who truly forgives are alike;
they both have set themselves free.

It's not natural to forgive someone who has hurt you, and it doesn't feel very safe or smart either, does it?

So, many couples live like two medieval knights who have agreed to a truce but wouldn't dream of removing their armor: *I'll never be vulnerable again and give you another opportunity to hurt me.* It makes sense, in a way . . . but is this what God intends for your marriage?

No wife should trust a husband who repeatedly sins

against her, offers a quick "I'm sorry" and then never changes, continuing to live as he did before. You can be civil and respectful, but trust? No.

But we're talking about a wife forgiving her husband when there is genuine turning from sin and forgiveness sought.

At first, refusing to forgive feels like you are protecting your heart from further injury. However, the unforgiving heart doesn't realize that this "safe place" is really a prison, surrounded by strong bars. Yes, you're safe, in a manner of speaking; but those bars provide the ideal environment for bitterness to do its worst in your soul, hollowing you out from the inside.

The offenses against you are not invented. They are real. But keep in mind what Jesus Christ taught about your kind of situation.

Jesus warns His followers – including wives and husbands – that if we won't forgive the small sins of others against us (small compared to the sins Jesus Christ carried for us on the cross), we most certainly will not be forgiven for our own sins.

An unforgiving spirit is serious business for the here-and-now, with the loneliness, hardness, and bitterness it brings, but also for eternity . . . especially for eternity.

Jesus wants you to forgive. Forgiveness is an *offering* because it's going to cost you something, but it's the way of wisdom for your marriage.

Forgive your spouse because you've been forgiven

– offering your spouse the same mercy and grace Jesus Christ has offered you. Then you'll discover that emptiness and bitterness can never grow in a forgiving heart.

> "Bearing with one another, and forgiving one another, if anyone has a complaint against another; even as Christ forgave you, so you also must do." (Colossians 3:13)

Dear Lord,

I don't want to have an unforgiving heart. I know how destructive it is to harbor such thoughts, and You've been very clear in Your Word that unwillingness to forgive has drastic eternal consequences. Please help me never to harbor bitterness in my heart. Help me to have the courage to either overlook an offense or the courage to speak directly and plainly about how I have been hurt. Lord, please protect our marriage from the practice of unforgiveness.

In Jesus' name, amen.

CHALLENGE:

If you know your husband wants you to forgive him for something, offer him sincere forgiveness for that hurt right now. If there are no outstanding debts to forgive, tell him that you'd love to go for a walk with him just to enjoy the open air together.

Notes

Notes

5
Breathing Life
by Lisa

A wise woman breathes life into her home by choosing cheerful words over complaining ones.

It all started with a sigh. A sigh so natural to me that I never noticed it escaping my lips.

A long heavy sigh.

I was washing vegetables for the dinner salad. Celery, peppers, and carrots. The typical evening prep. Feeling behind and burdened by my day.

That's when my husband walked into the room and asked, "Hey, babe, how was today?" And then, "Why the big sigh?"

He asked and so I answered. And it went something like this:

"The bickering kids, the avalanche of housework, the unanswered emails, the half-broken appliances, the errands that took longer than they should have, and the three medical bills that arrived in the mail . . . ."

A long list of complaints, but nothing special. All the usual.

But right before my eyes, I watched those strong, solid shoulders of the man I love drop a little. Hunch over a bit. Heavy with all I'd just dumped on him.

But he'd asked and I'd answered him honestly. And I believe it's important to be honest, don't you?

Except for one thing.

My "honesty" was taking him down. I was literally sucking the life out of our home with my complaining. I'd developed the very bad habit of grumbling, and I'd masked it all under the disguise of "being honest" instead of calling what it really was.

What *I* really was.

A complaining wife.

And that's when I knew something had to change. I had to stop this negative stream of communication that greeted him almost every evening. It was time to trade out my whining discontent and to replace it with a thankful spirit. To choose cheerful words rather than negative ones.

I wanted to breathe life back into my home and our relationship.

Oh, not that it meant I could never be "honest" again; there's a time and place for that. But I realized that I could save it for another moment. And I was going to make sure that I wasn't merely "dumping" on him, but truly coming to him for support, help, or a little sympathy. Not complaining for the sake of complaining.

Rather than focusing on all that had gone wrong, I was going to concentrate on all that was good in my day. Things that were true, lovely, and worthy.

And that goes something like this:

"The kids had lots of fun at the park today, I got the pantry cleaned out, so glad for my washing machine and (partially-working) dryer, made it to the grocery store, got a nice compliment from my co-worker, and grateful our girl got medical care when she really needed it . . . ."

Same day – different perspective. And that has made all the difference in the world.

Maybe you've picked up the habit of complaining as well? Try changing this one bad habit and see the good it brings to your husband, your marriage, and your home.

Dear Lord,

I never, ever want to be a wife known for her inclination to complain. Help me to see the good that is in my life because of Your grace, and to see the good in my husband, family, friends, and opportunities. I know mature, godly women are not complainers. Please do Your work in me.

In Jesus' name, amen.

ASK YOUR HUSBAND:

"Are there any topics that come up where you see that I drift into negative conversation? Please know that I am determined to grow in this area. I never want you to feel that your wife is a complainer. There are so many things about my life with you that I deeply appreciate."

Notes

Notes

6

The Pleasure of Intimacy

by Matthew

When it comes to making love, only the birds and bees should consider sex as merely a task.

There's nothing like a wife "doing her duty" in the bedroom to throw cold water on the fires of passion.

Yes, there are two sides – two spheres of responsibility – in this aspect of marriage but we're not talking about him right now.

If your duty is all you are willing to do, he might settle for it, but inside he'll never be satisfied with your sex life. He wants more than mere sex. He wants you – body, mind, and spirit.

You may be physically there, in the bedroom, but he

can tell instantly when your mind and spirit are somewhere else. What is the message you're sending when you are uninvolved?

Here's what he is thinking:

She's not enjoying this.

She wants me to stop.

She doesn't find me physically appealing.

I must be doing it wrong.

Maybe I don't have what it takes to arouse her.

Are these the messages you wish to send every time the two of you turn out the lights?

Maybe you genuinely don't feel much of anything. Don't let yourself believe that is the way it has to remain. God intended for you to feel intense enjoyment – and for your husband to experience this with you.

Has it ever occurred to you that you can pray about sex – even when you are in the middle of the act? God won't blush. Ask God to help you to enter more deeply into the experience.

Then . . .

Ask your husband if the two of you can talk about sex. There's a guaranteed way to get his attention! Ask him if he is interested in hearing from you the kinds of things that make you feel close to him, that arouse you, and that you would enjoy the next time the two of you come together.

You might want to explain to him, for example, that it takes you a little time to get prepared, whereas he can be ready in 1.5 seconds!

Maybe draw the curtains, wear something pretty, or run a bubble bath to help you meet him where he is. Maybe he will enjoy being a part of the preparations, and some sexual creativity will start to happen.

Then . . .

Don't leave any stone unturned. Some women may not even know how much past sexual promiscuity or abuse is affecting their lives now. Christ has healing for your past. But first, you must acknowledge what may be happening in your mind and find support for bringing this to the surface. Always include your husband in the process; it will bring you closer together.

Dear Lord,

I confess, there have been times when all I have wanted to do is my "duty" in the bedroom. Please help me to understand this isn't what I am called to do, that my husband wants so much more than that. Please give me the desire to be fully engaged in our lovemaking. Help me to communicate to him that I desire to be with him and to enjoy our intimate times.

Lord, please give me an increased desire for my husband.

In Jesus' name, amen.

Ask your husband:

"Is there anything I do when we have sex that you especially enjoy? Is there anything that you'd like me to do? I want to hear it and I would like to share some things that I would enjoy trying. Please know it is my desire to be with you and not only to fulfill my duty but to be completely involved with you, at every level, when we make love."

Notes

Notes

7
Respecting Him
by Lisa

*A wise woman makes healthy deposits of respect
into her husband's soul account.*

I'm sure Paul thought he made it simple enough in
Ephesians 5:33: "Let the wife see that she respects her
husband."

Except that this respect thing isn't quite as clear as I'd like
it to be.

Not like love. I know what it looks like to love. That's
an easy one.

Love is when he spends time with me. Listens to me.
Cares about me. Looks after me. Takes a keen interest in
my thoughts and ideas.

No, love is any easy one to figure out.

But *respect?* That's an entirely different matter.

Apparently, it's an important matter, though. So important that you'll find respect toward the top of his list. Yes, respect is highly-rated among the men. I've even heard it said they would rather be unloved than disrespected – is that wild or what?

Now the fact is that I *do* respect my husband. I honestly do. I guess it's the showing of it that gets to be something of a challenge. Because you've heard how we each have our own unique "love language"?

Well, I suspect there must be some kind of "respect language" too. You know, "what says respect to him" or something along those lines.

So one day I just up and asked him. Straight out. "What makes you feel respected? By me?" And I waited for his answer.

And waited.

After a while, he mentioned a thing or two. Things like how I'll talk positively about him in public. Or how I'll *ask* him to do something, rather than order him around about what needs to be done to the house. Then he added that he likes how I'll stop what I'm doing to greet him when he comes in the door.

These were meaningful things to him. But for the most part? I was on my own.

I made it a point to study what made him smile, as well as what made him flinch. It was up to me to figure out what made him feel respected.

So why not ask your own husband what makes him feel respected?

Take to heart whatever he shares with you and then add to that list from what you're able to learn by watching him. Pray about it and ask God to show you the ways you can lovingly respect your husband.

You might be surprised to see what a difference it makes in your marriage.

Dear Lord,

I pray You'll help me to see the various ways I can show respect to my husband, as well as to see any way that I've shown disrespect to him. I want to communicate the kind of respect I'm called to give him. Help me to be more aware of what my voice, my words, and my actions say about my regard for him.

In Jesus' name, amen.

ASK YOUR HUSBAND:

"Do you feel respected by me? Is there anything I can do – or not do – to better communicate respect to you?"

Notes

Notes

8
Kind Words
by Matthew

*Regularly speaking kind and loving words
brings the spirit of peace into your home.*

How do you talk to your husband in normal, everyday communication? Is your speech marked by soft, loving words?

What would your husband say if he were asked, "Does your wife communicate with you in a kind manner?"

Choosing to communicate with kindness and love in marriage is a spiritual discipline. We're so wired to respond "in the same manner" that whenever a perceived provocation of any degree is felt, we react on autopilot.

When challenging moments happen, you need to be

ready, having prepared yourself with the truth that you are not the victim of your fleshly impulses. You have the power to respond, in any situation, with a soft answer.

But what about all those other moments that fill the normal days of marriage? Are you speaking lovingly then? Consider these examples:

"Hey, take out the trash," versus, "Hey, babe, I'd love it if you could take out the trash . . . I sure appreciate you!"

"The doctor's bill came. You need to pay it," versus, "Is this a good time to talk about some bills that have come in?"

"On your way home, pick up some milk and eggs," versus, "Hey, love, would you mind picking up some milk and eggs on the way home?"

When mundane things are referenced with kindness and love you are actually adding a layer of respect to your conversation.

You may have different discussions in your home, but the principle is the same. When you speak – even in the small, seemingly insignificant matters that make up the day – do so in a thoughtful manner. Peace follows a soft approach. After all, it's difficult to have strife with a person who is speaking to you in a gentle tone. Purpose to be a woman who speaks kindly toward your husband.

> "And be kind to one another, tenderhearted, forgiving one another, even as God in Christ has forgiven you." (Ephesians 4:32)

Dear Lord,

I desire to be known as a wife who speaks soft words. Please fill my heart with love, so that when I speak, kindness and love are what comes out and our home is filled with peace.

In Jesus' name, amen.

ASK YOUR HUSBAND:

"Can you think of something I often say to you that you wish were cushioned with a little more kindness? I really want to make an effort to change that."

Notes

9
Living A Love Story
by Lisa

*The wise wife confidently encourages her children
to follow her example in marriage.*

You don't realize how much they're watching.

Or at least not how *closely* they're watching.

Because even though I thought I knew how much it
meant to them, it wasn't until a recent discussion that I
found out just how much our kids carefully take note of
our marriage.

Our daughter came home from her freshmen year
at college for a quick visit and started telling me about a
conversation she'd had with one of her guy friends.

And it wasn't what I would have expected.

She casually mentioned to him, "Yeah, I'd call my parents right now but I can't because they're out on a date."

"What do you mean? I thought they were married?"

Our daughter started laughing. "Um, yes, they're definitely married. Like for over 24 years now."

"So why would they be dating?" He was baffled but wanted to understand.

"I don't know; they're often going out on dates."

He thought about it for a minute or two. "I'm not sure my parents have ever gone on a date. Not that I can remember, at least."

And then he added, "And I only saw them holding hands a few times in my entire life." The young man was nineteen years old.

Now she was the one confused. "That's strange. My parents are all over each other."

She said that. She said we were "all over each other."

Okay, so it's a bit embarrassing to hear your teenage daughter describing you as basically "hot for one another," and I had to stop her at this point in the story.

"You didn't actually say that, did you?"

"Yeah, of course, I did. What? You thought we kids didn't notice? But I didn't realize that having that kind of marriage is so rare. Few – if any – of my friends' parents have that sort of relationship. Kinda weird, huh?"

I don't know if I'd use the word "weird" or not, but it does seem a little sad.

After all, our daughter attends a Christian college, so you'd think that would be *the best* place to hear about healthy, wonderful, and *passionate* marriages.

But she said it's *rare*.

Obviously, there are even better reasons to have a great marriage than for the sake of college students' conversation.

God calls us to love deeply. He desires us to have more than a functional marriage. It's a beautiful testimony of love to the world. And, besides, it's a lovely way to live.

But how about considering this as well? Our children are watching us. They're learning how to love other people by seeing how we love one another. They're studying our example on what it means to be married and what their marriage should (or should not) look like.

Our kids want us – need us – to have an ongoing love story.

Give your kids something to talk about. And you might find out they're still talking about it long after they've left home.

Are you living a love story?

Dear Lord,

I want to show our children how a loving marriage looks. I realize they're watching and learning from our relationship, and I want to give them the kind of example that honors You. I know they don't need "perfect," but I hope and pray that we demonstrate love above all.

In Jesus' name, amen.

TALK TO YOUR HUSBAND:

Sit down and ask your husband what kind of relationship he thinks you both demonstrate to your children. Discuss together the different ways that you can be more loving or demonstrative in front of them.

Notes

Notes

10
Helping Him

by Matthew

*Embracing what God has said about your
helping role in marriage brings blessing,
peace, and order to your home.*

A good husband will help his wife in many wonderful
ways. But the husband is not designated "helper" in
the marriage by God; the wife is.

Do you see yourself as your husband's helper?

The idea of being a helper strikes some as a secondary
status, but if God described a wife's role that way, is it
really a put-down?

. . . And is that how God described it?

In Genesis 2:18 (NASB), God did describe it that way. He said, "'. . . I will make him a helper suitable for him.'" A "suitable" helper – why did God say that? He had given Adam a monumental responsibility and nothing in all of creation was found that could help him succeed. There was no possibility of him fulfilling that responsibility without help . . . without a woman . . . without a wife.

Your husband cannot fulfill his calling without you by his side, standing strong, helping him in life. God designed it that way and God's design is always the best and most beautiful.

Many marriages struggle greatly because the husband and wife haven't settled on the biblical order and structure of their relationship. Like a car where two people try to drive at the same time, disorder follows.

When we marry, we enter into a single entity; the two have become one. Within that single entity, God's best is realized by embracing God's way. God has ascribed the role of "suitable helper" to the wife. Will you embrace God's perspective for His best in your marriage?

Dear Lord,

I want my husband to feel my full support and understanding of our relationship. Help me to keep in mind the reality of how You have structured marriage. Help me to remember that I am honored to be given the role as helper to him in our home and family.

In Jesus' name, amen.

ASK YOUR HUSBAND:

"In Genesis 2:18, God says that Eve was created to be Adam's helper. I'm asking God to help me take this seriously. If you could name three things that would cause you to feel my support as the helper that God created for you, what would they be?"

Notes

11
The Small Things
by Lisa

*The wise wife prevents small things
from becoming big things by caring about
the details that matter to her husband.*

ow can one jar of peanut butter cause so much
trouble?

That's what I wanted to know. Because apparently, it
was a big problem. He made that quite clear.

My husband was fed up with the sticky, slimy mess
dripping down the sides of the peanut butter jar and
insisted that we put a stop to the madness. "Why can't we

keep this jar clean?! There's no reason we should live like this, and it's driving me nuts!"

He didn't yell, but I could tell by his tone that he really meant it.

Oh, but there was a very good reason as far as I was concerned, and I protested his somewhat ridiculous request.

There were actually *eight* good reasons. You see, we have eight children and one mother can hardly be expected to keep on top of everything. They all make their own peanut butter sandwiches. Even the three youngest boys. Why so unreasonable? So demanding?

Now on his behalf, I have to tell you that my husband is not a complainer. He doesn't make negative remarks about my cooking. He doesn't complain about having to throw on his robe in the morning and search for essential items in the laundry room. He's even good about patiently sitting in the car and waiting for me to get out the front door. And that can be a pretty long wait sometimes.

But the goopy peanut butter container? That just about does him in.

And I basically communicated to him, "Sorry. But that's just the way it has to be." That we were going to have to learn to live with it. That he was asking the impossible.

I left him in the kitchen, feeling quite justified in my defensive and somewhat huffy response.

Except for one thing . . .

I left the kitchen to recover and regroup in our front

sitting room – our "parlor," as we call my very favorite room in the house. It's my special place; in the parlor, we have pretty pillows, a tea tray, and a *clear glass* coffee table.

The kids are not allowed to eat in this room. No electronic gadgets, either. No LEGO® bricks, dirty socks, or rollerblades are permitted in the parlor.

I love this room.

So are you beginning to wonder how it is that I can keep an entire room looking pristine even though we have eight children? With a glass coffee table, no less?

Well, it's because it's important to me. *Really important.*

But I can't keep the peanut butter jar wiped down?

Right. That's the question that got to me too. You see, I have this tendency to take my priorities very seriously. And this room is one of those. Not only that but when the rest of my family does their best to keep it the way I like it?

It makes me happy. I feel respected. Maybe even loved.

I know. It's a small thing.

But it's a big deal to me to keep my parlor perfect, if at all possible.

So maybe I don't understand why all the fuss over the sloppy peanut butter jar. But if it's important to him? Makes him happy? Feel respected? Maybe even *loved . . .* ?

Then I can do this one small thing. In fact, I'm determined to have the cleanest peanut butter jar in town.

And if your husband also has those "little things" that

bother him? Consider the ways you can make them your priority, too.

"Let each of you look out not only for his [or her] own interests, but also for the interests of others." (Philippians 2:4)

Dear Lord,

I want to get better at showing my husband that those things that matter to him matter to me, too. Show me how I can look after him in ways that mean a lot to him, even if they don't make as much sense to me. Help me to be more generous with my time and efforts, showing him that he is truly a priority to me.

In Jesus' name, amen.

ASK YOUR HUSBAND:

"What are some of those little things that you've asked me to take care of but that I've blown off?" Then let him know that you want to work on making his small preferences more of your priority.

Notes

12

The Gift of Gratitude

by Matthew

*A single ounce of gold in a poor country
and a little gratitude in marriage are alike;
they both go a long way.*

*E*veryone wants to be valued. Everyone wants to be appreciated.

When was the last time you looked your husband in the eyes and sincerely expressed, "I'm so grateful for . . ." or "I really appreciate you because . . ."?

What is there to be grateful for?

Did you have breakfast this morning?

Is there heat in the house in winter?

Does he protect your family?

Is he faithful to you?

Does he play with the kids?

Is he kind?

Did he unplug the toilet?

Does he come home to you at the end of every work day?

Every wife has good reasons to be grateful, even if it takes some effort to think of those reasons.

But being grateful isn't enough. We must express our gratefulness, in order for it to have meaning and power.

In our home, we often talk about how, when there is a lack of appreciation from a spouse, we immediately *assume* the worst. Not only do we not feel appreciated, but we start imagining that the person may be thinking critically about us. It's human nature.

You wouldn't say you've been taking him for granted, would you? Certainly not intentionally! But that's how a lack of expressed appreciation works. We're just busy and don't take the time to communicate.

Most men won't say anything. They'll just keep soldiering on, but what a refreshing drink the smallest word of appreciation can be.

The power of gratefulness runs both directions – to the giver and to the receiver. Being grateful means you're going to have a great day! It's impossible to be annoyed and miserable when you're grateful.

When you express sincere gratitude, it starts a powerful, positive communication cycle and builds value in the heart of your husband. It binds his heart to yours.

Are you a thankful, grateful wife?

> "In everything give thanks; for this is the will of God in Christ Jesus for you." (1 Thessalonians 5:18)

Dear Lord,

Please help me to exude a spirit of gratitude for my husband. I pray he will feel like he's married to the most grateful woman he's ever met — that he truly feels my appreciation for him on a daily basis.

In Jesus' name, amen.

CHALLENGE:

Tell your husband three things that he does on a regular basis that you appreciate but realize you haven't ever expressed thankfulness for.

Notes

Notes

13

A Sweet Response

by Lisa

Responding with sweetness when it isn't deserved places love where it isn't expected.

I recently had one of those difficult days.

Or, to be more accurate, I had a difficult *week*. And I was close to tears by late afternoon.

Matthew came into the room and asked me what was wrong and I hate to say it, but I snapped at him.

He stared at me and I felt a bit of guilt for the hurt I saw there. I was taking it out on him and he didn't deserve it.

But I was not feeling guilty enough to apologize. I was too wrapped up in my own struggles.

I figured it was about to get ugly and, frankly, I had asked for it with my snotty attitude.

Then I saw his countenance visibly change – from offended to compassionate. He didn't exactly understand where I was coming from, but then again, he didn't need to. What mattered was that I was in a bad place.

His eyes softened. He reached out with a gentle touch. Asked me if I'd like to run into town with him. A mini-errand date.

He also announced to the kids that Mommy was turning in early that night. And then later ran a bubble bath for me.

So yes, I did end up crying that evening, but these were very different tears. They were the tears that come when someone shows kindness to you that you didn't necessarily deserve.

My husband is the hero in this story. But you know what? I learned something anew. I was reminded of the power of offering a sweet response in our marriage.

When your husband is having one of those days or one of those weeks, sometimes you don't need to say anything at all. You can just look at your husband with loving eyes and communicate that you care and that you'll always be there. Maybe reach for his hand or rub his knotted shoulders – all small gestures that can have a powerful effect on the man you love.

It's even possible to completely turn around a tense situation by returning harsh or unjust words with a sweet response.

So I don't know about you, but I've renewed my commitment to show kindness to my husband. Even those times when he doesn't necessarily deserve it. Maybe even *especially* in those times.

"A soft answer turns away wrath." (Proverbs 15:1)

Dear Lord,

I want to show kindness to my husband. Give me a soft heart toward him so that I can respond sweetly, even in those times when he's not being sweet to me. I pray that You will fill me with the love and compassion that can only come from You. Help me to learn to speak and act kindly toward him, no matter what the circumstances

In Jesus' name, amen.

CHALLENGE:

If you're convicted in how you've spoken or acted toward your husband, take the time to ask his forgiveness. Let him know you repent of your harshness – or even meanness – and that you are committed to growing in kindness toward him.

Notes

Notes

14

No Secrets

by Matthew

*The wise wife strips past secrets of their power
by bringing them into the light.*

You want to be close to him, and you are. The two of
you have a good relationship, but every once in a while,
a nagging thought creeps from somewhere out of the
past and torments you. *What if he knew about . . . that?*

Secrets from the past wield an immense power in the
mind of the person they torment and, consequently, in the
peace you have in your marriage. Every time you imagine
him finding out your secret, a cold chill crawls up your
spine. *I just couldn't let him find out. It would hurt him so much.
Would he even forgive me?*

Sin brings shame, pain, and consequences. Telling your husband involves risk because you don't know how he will respond.

What would God have you do?

Consider His will for your marriage:

> ". . . and the two shall become one flesh." (Mark 10:8)

To experience the fullness of true intimacy and oneness, you cannot keep secrets from your husband. Ask God to give you the courage to bring into the light the matter that has plagued you with anxiety in the darkness.

Whenever we bravely bring sin into the light, we discover how powerless it really is. The chains that you felt for so long begin to loosen their hold, often more quickly than you thought possible.

Is there something from which God wants you to be free today? Don't keep secrets from one another. Remove their power by bringing them into the light.

Dear Lord,

You know everything about me – every good and bad thing. I want my husband and me to get to that place of total transparency. May there be no shadows from the past to haunt our future. Please help me to be honest, open, and vulnerable with my husband with every aspect of my life. I also pray that I would be the kind of wife who provides such a safe, loving, open spirit toward my husband that if there are any things haunting him from his past, he would know he can trust me with them.

In Jesus' name, amen.

CHALLENGE:

Sharing a secret could be one of the most difficult conversations to ever approach . . . but it could also be the most freeing one you ever have with your husband. If you have fear about this, you are in good company! Humanly speaking, you are not alone. The real key is this: spiritually speaking, you are not alone. You can ask God's Holy Spirit to give you strength. Seek counsel if you need it, but determine that you will get to a place where you share these secrets with your husband.

Notes

15
Lasting Friendship

by Lisa

*There is no marriage so warm and close as two
deep friends sharing life together.*

He often introduces me as his girlfriend.

It's ever-so-slightly embarrassing.

He'll say it to the barista at the cafe, or to the cashier in the checkout line at the grocery store. After 24 years, you'd think I'd get used to it, but it still makes me blush. And smile.

I always hurry to add that I also happen to be his wife – an important fact to establish when you have eight children together. And I'll flash my wedding ring to prove it, if necessary.

I think he gets some odd gratification out of my embarrassment. Then he'll pretend to protest, "What? You are my girlfriend, aren't you?"

Yes, well . . .

It's true. I am a girl. And I am his friend. A close friend. The best of friends, really.

I guess that makes me his girlfriend. And like most good friendships, ours has grown over time. We've had to invest in our friendship and look after it.

So many times, people think it's because we somehow "click." But while there might be some "clicking" between us, it's more than that. Far more than that.

Our friendship is a long, purposeful process.

So how do you build a friendship with your husband?

Honestly? It's not much different than any other friendship. It requires spending time together. It means sharing interests and having fun together. It involves praying for him and being thoughtful toward him. Just doing the kinds of things that friends do for one another.

Dear Lord,

Help me to communicate closely with my husband every day, as a good friend would. May my face light up when he walks in the room. Give me an understanding of how to share in his interests. Help me to remember to tell him I like him. When all the world feels like an enemy, help him feel the safe warmth of my friendship.

In Jesus' name, amen.

CHALLENGE:

Tell your husband you like him. Ask if you can go out on an ice cream date, just to talk about what you enjoy doing together as friends. Make some fun plans!

Notes

16

The Kingmaker

by Matthew

*The woman who builds up her husband in public
will soon find she is married to a king.*

You are a kingmaker. Do you realize that?

Proverbs 31 is clear. The reason the husband of the Proverbs 31 Woman is respected in the gate – in public, among his peers – is because of how his wife conducts herself.

There is one area where every wife has an opportunity to make her husband feel like a king: how she interacts with him in public.

We've all observed a wife tearing down her husband in the company of others. When a wife openly and regularly contradicts her husband in conversation with others, whether intentionally or not, she is diminishing him, herself, and their marriage.

But he was wrong about the trip; it was the first, not the second week in June. I was just setting the record straight.

No, that happened when Johnny was eight not nine. He always gets the facts wrong!

It's almost always unnecessary to correct your husband in public. So why is it happening?

I'm smart when it comes to the details. I remember the facts better than he does. Why shouldn't I be part of the conversation, too?

Being part of the conversation and cutting down your husband in front of others are not the same thing. Cutting down your husband is exactly what is happening when you repeatedly correct and contradict him.

Yes, you're smart, but do you have humility?

If there is a crucial bit of information that absolutely needs correcting, the discreet, wise wife will find a moment to take her husband aside privately and tell him respectfully.

Is your husband respected – in public, by the people you know – because of how you conduct yourself? Do you resist the impulse to correct him before others?

Remember, you are a kingmaker. It's how God designed marriage. Use your power wisely.

> "Her husband is known in the gates,
> when he sits among the elders of the land."
> (Proverbs 31:23)

Dear Lord,

Help me never to contradict my husband in public, either directly with words or indirectly by a disapproving look.

In Jesus' name, amen.

ASK YOUR HUSBAND:

"Do I contradict you in front of others? Have I ever shown a lack of support by giving you a disapproving look when we are with others?"

Notes

17
Communicating Love

by Lisa

*A wise wife recognizes and appreciates
the different ways love is expressed to her.*

*H*ave you ever had a week where it's been just one thing after another?

We had one of those not too long ago and it started out with an unusually rugged winter storm. And wouldn't you know it, but it also happened to be the week that my husband was out of town.

Now, I'm not exactly known as a pioneer woman around here, but I was determined to be tough in this near-arctic situation. "I can do this," I told him. And he believed me.

Until the pump in the well froze up. Which means no water.

But don't worry, that didn't get me down. I've read *Little House on the Prairie*, so I knew just what to do. Melt snow over the stove and *ta-da!* Water. I felt so very resourceful and pioneer-ish.

Until later in the day when the propane ran out. Which meant no heat. So there we all were – the kids and me – huddled around our fireplace and trying to keep warm. They loved it!

Me, less so. Especially when I realized that no propane means no hot water which means *no shower* – unless you're a member of the Polar Bear Club which I am *not*.

Finally, at the end of this unusually long week, my husband crossed the winter storm and returned home to us. He swept me up in his arms, kissing me and telling me how proud he was of my strength and bravery under such trying conditions . . .

No, wait.

That's not what happened.

He came into the house and – hero that he is – immediately started making calls to see about getting our road plowed as we were quite buried in snow by that point.

And me? I fell apart.

I was tired and discouraged, and my feelings were hurt that he hadn't kissed me when he got home. Not only that, but I wanted to hear from him what an amazing job I'd done while he was away. *I wanted to hear how much he loved me.*

He stared at me while I shared all this, watching my eyes fill with tears. "But, baby, I was loving you."

I tried again. "What? You didn't even kiss me when you came in the door!"

He attempted to explain it another way, "You see, when I'm getting those roads plowed, in my mind, I *am* loving you. With all my heart. I'm looking after you and that's my way of saying, 'I love you.'"

I forced myself to think about this for a minute. Seemed a little silly to me. How can "plowing snow" possibly substitute for a sweeping kiss? And what about a glowing tribute to what an incredible wife I was for holding down the fort under such stressful conditions?

But I could tell he was sincere.

So, I laughed. Mostly at myself. And eventually thanked him for "loving me" by getting our road plowed. Romantic, I suppose, in a pioneering sort of way.

How about you? Have you ever had a moment – or multiple moments – when his love didn't look exactly how you imagined it would be? But if you really thought about it from his perspective, he was sincerely trying to show love to you in his own way.

Open your eyes to see that he's genuinely trying. That even if he's not following the script you've set out for him, it still counts as love.

Not that there's anything wrong with communicating what would be meaningful to you. Not that you can't say, "Hey, what about kissing me straight on the lips?" or, "I could sure use some affirming words here, babe!"

But then wrap your arms around each other and be content to watch the snowplow run up and down your country road.

It can be terribly romantic. If only you have the eyes to see it.

Dear Lord,

I pray that You help me recognize the special ways that my husband shows love for me — even when they are different than the ways that I'd hoped for or imagined. I pray that You'll open my eyes to the little things that he says or does that demonstrate his love and that I would learn to appreciate them.

In Jesus' name, amen.

Ask your husband:

"What are some of the little ways that you show love to me that I don't always see? Are there times that I impose my own definition of love onto you and make you feel like I don't appreciate you?"

Notes

18

A Beautiful Submission

by Matthew

A wise woman embraces the protection, pleasure, and prosperity that comes with submitting to her husband.

ubmit to Jesus?

We'll check that box on the multiple-choice exam every time. No problem (we say!), Jesus is good, righteous, just, merciful, and possesses all power and authority. And, He loves us so much!

But then there's the s-word directed to wives about their own husbands.

Submit to *him*? Not so fast.

Some wives have legitimate reasons not to submit to

the men they are married to, but these are exceptions, not the norm. What is normal for biblical order in Christian marriage? When it comes to reading your own mail – the parts of the Bible directed to you – do you understand the order of authority?

Ephesians 5:22 could hardly be clearer. In marriage, a wife submitted to her husband is God's standard. And, in a marriage where a man has truly laid down his life for his wife, submission is beautiful and safe.

How is that possible? Because of Jesus – the Bridegroom of the Church.

Biblical submission isn't yielding to your husband's will. Biblical submission is embracing the order Christ established and submitting to Him. That's what the phrase, "as unto the Lord," means in Ephesians 5:22.

Embracing biblical order in marriage is service to Christ, not subservience to your husband.

Jesus is the perfect Head of the Church, His bride. Does His perfection make the Church's response to Him consistently holy, right, and yielded? No, because despite His perfection, we all still struggle against our flesh.

And so it is in marriage. Having the perfect husband will not make you the perfect wife. We know neither of us is perfect, yet God still calls us to walk in His established biblical order.

What does that look like in your home?

In every home, there will be variations of how this plays out, but in every Christian marriage where the couple is determined to walk in a biblical manner, the wife will seek to honor God by submitting to her husband's leadership.

Dear Lord,

My flesh hates submitting to anyone or anything, but I desire to enjoy the blessings of obedience found in Your Word. Lord, please do Your work in me, as I submit to You, to Your Word, and subsequently to my husband. May my marriage represent the beautiful oneness You intend for every marriage.

In Jesus' name, amen.

ASK YOUR HUSBAND:

"Can you help me remember a time when I submitted to your leadership and it was a wonderful experience for both of us? Is there an area in our lives in which you'd like me to be more submissive?"

Notes

Notes

19
In First Place

by Lisa

The wise wife loves her children by keeping her husband in first place in her heart.

You wouldn't have to know me for long to conclude that I'm a mom who is crazy about her kids.

I think about them. Pray for them. Make time for them. Talk to them. Listen to them. Laugh with them. Love on them.

Yep. Definitely a bit crazy.

In fact, I love my kids so much . . . that I'm willing to sweep them aside.

When their dad walks through that door.

They all know the drill. When Daddy returns home, everyone moves over to clear a path for what's about to take place. There's sure to be some hugging and kissing going on, so it's best to find something else to do if you don't want to watch the inevitable.

Ooh! Dad's here. And there goes Momma . . .

Because even though I love our children, my husband is first in my heart.

It's funny, but somehow our children don't mind much. They're good with taking second place. They don't feel rejected or denied (I actually think they kind of like it). Some giggle and others groan, yet overall, they're rather pleased with the way things are between him and me.

It means a lot to them when Dad and Mom love on each other. If they see us kiss, talk kindly, and laugh together? Then it's as though we're not only speaking love to each other, we're speaking love to them too.

When Momma stops everything she's doing to welcome Dad home? When she wraps her arms around his neck and smiles up at his face? When she makes caring for him her priority? It's showing our kids there's a lot of love in this home – love that can't help but overflow down to the rest of them.

When Dad and Mom love each other, it provides a warm, caring atmosphere in the home. This sets the tone for the entire family, and it lightens up everyone's heart to see two people loving each other.

So, if you're crazy about your kids? Well, so am I. But

no matter how caught up with your children you might be, don't leave out being crazy-in-love with their daddy, too.

Because loving him is one of the most loving things a mom can do.

Is your husband first in your heart, even before your relationship with your kids?

Dear Lord,

Help me never to cause my husband to feel he is being passed over because of too much focus and attention on our children. Help me to communicate to him that, next to You, he will always have first place in my heart.

In Jesus' name, amen.

ASK YOUR HUSBAND:

"Have I ever made you feel as if you are unimportant compared to the kids? Have you ever felt passed over? I never want you to feel that way."

Notes

Notes

20

Follow the Leader

by Matthew

She who gladly looks to her husband for spiritual leadership will watch a spiritual leader emerge before her very eyes.

Are you looking to your husband as the spiritual leader of your home?

Do you see yourself as following his leadership and direction? The Scriptures are clear on the topic: the husband is the spiritual head of the home.

Speaking of marriage, in 1 Corinthians 11:3, Paul says:

> "But I want you to know that the head
> of every man is Christ, the head of woman

is man, and the head of Christ is God."

So, regardless of how we think of the issue, the Bible declares that the husband is placed in the position of leadership, spiritually.

It's true, though, that you can't follow a parked car. This is frustrating for many women. *Will he ever lead?*

What's a wife to do?

The natural response to this vacuum is to fill it, and many wives – fed up and frustrated with the lack of leadership in their husbands – take the lead and act.

Is doing something better than doing nothing?

One thing is certain: the degree to which you, as a wife, take the leadership in your home is the degree to which your husband will never step up and assume his God-given responsibility to lead.

As tempting and seemingly necessary as it is to make something happen, there is a better way for those women who long to see their husbands lead spiritually. You have a great deal of power to act, but not in the seemingly obvious way of taking the reins of leadership.

First of all, it's imperative to see your husband as the spiritual leader, to believe it is God's design.

Go to your husband and tell him that you are following him. Tell him that you look to his spiritual leadership for you and for your family. This alone will come as a major shock to many husbands.

What? Me? I'm your spiritual leader and the head of this home? You're looking to me for leadership? Wow!

What's next? Now what should you do? It's a surprising answer but, you should do . . .

Nothing.

That's right, nothing. When it comes to leadership and spiritual direction, don't act. Don't take the lead. Yes, this will be difficult for the results-oriented woman, and it will require discipline. That's where the next step comes in.

Pray and put your hope in God. Immerse yourself in the love and providence of God. Believe that while God is working on your husband, He has a plan for your growth in His Spirit. You simply can never go wrong by taking the energy that you would have poured into trying to act as the spiritual leader of your home and turning this toward your own devotion to God.

And as you continue to do "nothing," focus on recognizing that your husband is the spiritual leader. As you pray and wait, something likely will happen – though not necessarily on your schedule.

You probably will not see it at first, and it will take time before he truly understands that you are sincere about following him, but with your words and support, his leadership muscles will start to twitch with a new sense of vigor.

You may be gifted with leadership. You may be tired of the inactivity and lack of spiritual direction. You may have an overpowering urge to act, to do *something*. God has a proper place for the use of your gifting, but, if you desire to see the spiritual leader in your husband emerge in your marriage, you must restrain yourself and stay out of the way.

Telling your husband that you are following him – truly submitted to his leadership in your marriage and home – is a message that comes with force and power.

Look to your husband for spiritual leadership and watch a spiritual leader emerge before your very eyes.

Dear Lord,

Help me to embrace the reality that I have a strong role to play in my husband's spiritual leadership of our relationship and home. Show me where I need to "back off" and wait patiently on You. Help me to rely on You for Your work in his heart and life. While You're working in his life, please reveal to me the areas where I can improve my own perspective, so that I clearly see my husband as my spiritual head and follow his lead.

In Jesus' name, amen.

TELL YOUR HUSBAND:

"I know the Bible is clear that you are my spiritual leader. I am determined to follow you and am excited about following your lead in our relationship and home."

Notes

21
Togetherness

by Lisa

The wise wife has banished the spirit of independence from her heart.

"**I** think it's pretty sweet . . . The way you always check in with your husband before committing to do most anything."

Sweet is not necessarily the word I would have used. But I do always "check in" with him. And he with me.

Because we've made it our practice to think and act as one.

Some people – like my friend – think it's sweet. It makes other people shudder. Like we're somehow just too "into" each other.

Do I ever feel stifled? Hindered? Slowed down by this whole "oneness" thing? Admittedly, it was a new way for me to look at life – this life we're now sharing together – but the Bible states that we are no longer two people like we were before.

We are now *one flesh*.

What exactly does that mean? Surely not simply that we sleep together. Not that it isn't important (because it is), but it's got to mean more than only that. One flesh is mentioned in such a way as not merely to be a matter of going to bed with him.

> "The two shall become one . . ."
> (Matthew 19:5)

No longer he and me . . . because now it's *we*. And you know what we've found? It takes a little – okay, a lot of – practice and intentionality. We have to purpose to think and act as one.

One of the ways that we practice unity is that we don't make independent decisions. We make all our major decisions together and run many minor ones by each other as well. And yes, I do believe in submitting to my husband because that's what God says in His Word (Ephesians 5:22). But at the same time, I'm blessed to be married to a man who values my opinion and cares deeply about my concerns. We aim to be of one mind as much as possible.

Another way we practice unity is by communicating our togetherness. That's the real reason why I "always check in with him." And maybe it is rather sweet. But it's more than that, too.

It's oneness and it's biblical; it's marriage.

No longer two.

But *one*.

Dear Lord,

Please help me to enjoy the sweet unity of making all my life decisions with my husband in mind. Teach me to be thoughtful of him and to live like we are a team, not like I am a single woman.

In Jesus' name, amen.

CHALLENGE:

Tell your husband how much you enjoy doing life with him. Make a commitment that you'll check with him before making any big plans.

Notes

Notes

22

As You Like It

by Matthew

Attending to your husband's small preferences returns far more than they cost to fulfill.

Preferences: every person has them. They're not "right'" or "wrong" – they just are.

Chocolate, butter pecan, or strawberry cheesecake ice cream?

Red or blue?

Blistering hot, black coffee or lukewarm coffee with cream and sugar?

A walk on the windy beach in winter or sitting by the fire with a good book?

Asian or Mexican food?

Sitting with your back to the wall or in the center of the restaurant?

When you were dating and during the first months of marriage, all those preferences and differences were endearing – things that made your husband interesting and lovable.

But, if you're not careful, after a few years of marriage, you can allow little differences to change from endearing to annoying.

I don't see why it's so important to heat the coffee cup before the coffee goes in.

On one level, your husband's preferences aren't important at all. If he gets everything the way he likes it or nothing the way he prefers, life will still go on. But, when it comes to growing deep in a relationship, your husband's preferences really matter – not because having or not having them fundamentally changes anything, but because of what your care in providing them says to him.

There is a message in your service.

In and of themselves, most preferences are trifles.

"Please close the bathroom door all the way when you come out."

"Make sure the garage door is closed when you leave."

"Would you not set your briefcase on the bed?"

But when you allow little likes and dislikes to become the "annoying" or "silly" demands of your spouse, they take on a whole new power. Suddenly your annoyances have given your spouse's preferences the power to degrade your marriage relationship and to begin the process of driving a wedge between his heart and yours.

That's sad because it's just not that difficult to accommodate your spouse in these small matters. It only becomes difficult because our attitude about them has changed . . . has become negative.

The good news is that you can change your attitude. And when you change your attitude, everything changes, as if a bright light were turned on in a dimly lit room.

What does it cost to bless your husband by *joyfully* serving him in the matter of small preferences? So very little.

Of course, you'd like your husband to reciprocate and lovingly attend to all your preferences and desires — serving him would then be easy, wouldn't it? But that's not how we're called to serve one another. Only doing good in proportion to the good done to us is a payback, not an acting out of love.

A wise woman seeks to serve with joy in the small preferences of her husband, not to get something in return, but to make her husband smile.

Dear Lord,

It's so easy to make small, insignificant acts seem like a huge burden. I don't want to be that kind of wife. Give me the heart, purpose, and resolve to serve my husband well, by being positive and ready to meet his preferences. In fact, help me to anticipate his small desires and surprise him by fulfilling them. Maybe he'll reciprocate and maybe he won't, but whatever the case help me to love him in the small preferences he has.

In Jesus' name, amen.

ASK YOUR HUSBAND:

"What are your favorite little things that I do to serve you? I would like to do a better job at those, just to see you smile. Is there a favorite snack you wish I would keep stocked? A little habit you wish I would stop? Is there anything you would like me to start doing or to change that would make you feel more loved by me?"

Notes

Notes

23
The Controlling Wife

by Lisa

The wife who wants to help her husband does so best by stepping back from having all the controls.

"**A**ggressively helpful."

That's how she described herself.

I stared at her for a minute when I first heard her say it. Somewhat incredulous that there was a "term" for this kind of thing. Neither of us spoke as I tried to decide if she was joking or serious.

This is from our daughter who – among many things – is highly competent. She instinctively knows where things go and what to do next. She's naturally very efficient and makes sure things are done right.

I'd not heard it expressed like that before, but "aggressively helpful" sure made sense to me. Obviously, helpfulness is a wonderful quality. I mean, what could be better than a woman who understands what needs to be done . . . and how to do it? It could be considered a gift.

But as fascinating as this revelation was, it's what my still-quite-single daughter said next that really caught my attention. "We laugh at it now, Mom, my tendency to be a tad overly helpful. But I have to tell you . . .

"I want to be anything – *anything* – but a controlling wife."

And I knew immediately what she was talking about. I knew it because I have this same inclination. This same ability to be "aggressively helpful."

It looks something like this:

I know the best way to get to Costco. The quickest and most expedient route.

I know how we should spend our Saturday. Don't worry, I've got a plan.

I know what gifts we should get the family this Christmas. I even know what we can – or can't – afford.

I know what he's trying to say, and I'm ready to jump in and finish his sentence if necessary.

Basically, I know how we should spend our time, how we should spend our money, and what move we should make next. I can be extremely helpful that way.

Oh, you too?

But what does this "gift" look like in our marriage? Rather than a blessing, it can be downright destructive – whether it's our intention or not – because we disguise it as *helpful* when it's actually an impulse to control.

Not that you woke up this morning wondering, "Now how can I be a controlling wife today?" No, of course not. Your heart is in the right place. You just want *to help.*

Which is exactly why we can be rather blind to this fault of ours. When we picture a "controlling woman," we picture a wife who is going around the house telling her husband what to do all the time.

We would never do that.

At least not directly.

After all, that wouldn't be respectful. Or biblical. Or even nice. Yet we somehow excuse our actions because we've convinced ourselves that it's for the greater good. It's about what's wise. Or practical. Faster. Smarter. *Don't worry, we've got this.*

So, I don't know about you, but I want to be anything – *anything* – but a controlling wife.

If that means we get to Costco 10 minutes later on his route, let's go that way.

If we spend Saturday working on house projects instead of that family outing I'd planned, let's get it done.

If we spend more money – or less – on Christmas gifts that I thought necessary, we'll be okay.

And if he's trying to say something, just let the guy finish his thought!

Think about it. Ask yourself the hard questions.

Am I truly being helpful?

Or have I become a controlling wife?

Because sometimes the most helpful thing you can do is to help a little less.

Dear Lord,

You have given me many gifts, and I desire to use them well. But if I've become more than merely "helpful" and have turned into a controlling wife, will You show me where I need to lighten up? Help me to have more self-control where I have the impulse to jump in and take over in areas that are not mine to run.

In Jesus' name, amen.

CHALLENGE:

Talk to your husband and find out if there's one area where he wishes you would let loose of the reins.

Notes

24

Ready for Change

by Matthew

The wise wife doesn't focus on her husband's flaws.

Wen it comes to the faults of your husband, you're perceptive. You can see each and every one with clarity.

To notice the lesser qualities of others and to diminish our own is only natural. We're human, after all. But that's the problem. It *is* natural – natural to our sinful flesh.

You have a great justification for focusing on your husband's faults: you are going to give him the gift of making him a better version of himself!

Beware: when you take aim at your husband's faults, you're focusing in the wrong direction. What is most needed in these moments is a mirror.

When change is needed, where does the Bible say your attention should be placed? In Luke 6:42 (my paraphrase), Jesus asks, "... how can you say 'let me extract the small piece of straw out of your eye [just a moment while I correct you] when you can't even see the huge log in your own eye?' You hypocrite, first get the logjam out of your own eye and after you have that accomplished, you can see clearly to help someone else see their own [much smaller] shortcomings."

There are four reasons you should never try to change your husband:

1. You can't change another person. This involves a power beyond human effort.

2. You have plenty of areas in your own life that need attention.

3. It's God's job to change people, not yours.

4. Most husbands like their wives trying to change them as much as they like someone standing six inches from their ear banging pots together during the Super Bowl.

It may well be that your husband has serious areas in his life that need meaningful change, and there may be appropriate times when these things can be addressed in a fruitful manner. However, God wants you to habitually focus on your own need for growth, not your husband's. Not only that but when we consider God's standard for us all – "Be holy, for I am holy." (1 Peter 1:16) – we're quickly faced with the reality of our own deep need for change, growth, and sanctification.

Pray for your husband, that God's best would be realized in his life and heart. But focus a laser where you should: on the areas in which God is calling you to be conformed to Jesus Christ.

Dear Lord,

It's so easy and natural to my flesh to see the imperfection of others and to minimize my own shortcomings. I pray for Your work in me, to help me to remember that You have much work to do in my heart and life. Please help me to change where I look: from my husband's shortcomings to the places You want me to be conformed to the image of Christ

In Jesus' name, amen.

CHALLENGE:

Tell your husband: "Where I have been critical in the past and have minimized my own faults, I ask for your forgiveness. From now on, I'm asking God to help me keep my eyes on my own shortcomings and not to focus on areas in your life that I think need improving."

Notes

Notes

25
The Romantic Refuge

by Lisa

When the bedroom is transformed from "storage room" to "our refuge," romance takes center stage.

As a child, I was notorious for a messy, hurricane-styled bedroom.

But then I grew up and got married. And guess what?

I got to share my room with someone else and he didn't necessarily appreciate my "style" for our room. The tornado look just wasn't for him.

The messy look isn't exactly peaceful and it's certainly not romantic. Let's put it this way, there's nothing in the steamy *Song of Solomon* about calling to him from across the stacks of boxes and piles of clutter.

So something – or in this case, *someone* – needed to change. And I grew determined to make it happen.

Our room no longer could be a dumping ground for all my stuff.

The purpose of our bedroom had to change dramatically. Now this wasn't merely "my" place but *our* place. And it said something about the two of us.

Our room represented us and – maybe even more importantly – what I thought about us.

Crazy and chaotic? Disordered and disheveled?

That's not the statement I wanted to make.

On the contrary, I want our bedroom to be a place of refuge. A room for rest and refreshment. I want to create a small sanctuary where we can get away from the troubles and pressures of the world.

Doesn't that sound lovely?

And whether he says anything about it or not, he will think so, too.

So if you've made your bedroom into a convenient storage spot, do something differently. Find storage or a place to fold laundry anywhere else, but not your bedroom.

And then make cleaning your bedroom one of your top priorities. It will show him that this place – this special spot for the two of you – is important to you.

Turn your bedroom into the sacred place it is meant to be for you and your husband.

"I have found the one whom my soul loves." (Song of Solomon 3:4, paraphrased)

Dear Lord,

I want the message I send to my husband — through how I organize and clean our bedroom — to be unmistakable. I want him to know, without a single doubt, that I love and care for our marriage and the sacred, private space of our bedroom. Help me never to use our bedroom as if it's merely a space like any other. Help me to be a good steward of the message I'm sending to my husband (and all others who see it!), by keeping our bedroom free of clutter.

In Jesus' name, amen.

Ask your husband:

"Are there any changes you would like me to make in how our bedroom is cared for and decorated?" Let him know that you care deeply how he feels about the private space you share with him.

Notes

Notes

26
More Than Sorry

by Matthew

A brilliantly cut 20-carat diamond
and a wife who apologizes are alike;
they're both rare and exceedingly valuable.

*I*t's not easy to forgive.

But for many wives, what is ten times harder than forgiving *is asking for forgiveness.*

We hear from Christian husbands over and over again, "My wife *never* apologizes to me, ever." What is typical is to let the "bad weather pass" and just carry on as if sinfulness never took place.

Does this describe you? Have you and your husband sinned against each other in the past three months, either in large or small ways? Have you asked him for forgiveness in the last three months?

It's hard to apologize, but it's important to remember that Jesus said, "Take up your cross daily and follow me." It might be helpful to remember what a cross is for; it's for putting the flesh to death. And who really wants that? Certainly not the typical Christian wife.

But you're not typical. You're a wife who is seeking to walk in the wisdom of biblical marriage. You want your marriage to grow deep and rich and full. For that to happen, it is imperative to regularly ask for forgiveness, from a genuine, contrite heart.

What does asking for forgiveness look like?

When we enter this arena, it's natural to look for equal guilt, but that's not the attitude of a repentant heart. That's pride talking, even though your husband has to face up to his own responsibility for his attitudes and actions. The truly penitent wife isn't interested in the guilt of her husband; she only desires to be absolved of her own guilt.

And just saying, "I'm sorry," doesn't get the job done. It's an incomplete apology.

A quick "sorry" is often a tactic for avoiding the shame of having to ask for forgiveness. Instead, humble yourself before your husband and say, "I'm sorry for [whatever you did, without mincing words]. Will you please forgive me?" In doing this, you make yourself vulnerable, in a position of supplication to someone who could deny your request, but shouldn't.

That's humbling – which is what Jesus wants for you. Remain humble regardless of your husband's response. Maybe he will share forgiveness with you right away or maybe not, but the outcome isn't your concern. You've done what is right and need to leave the rest in God's hands.

Hopefully, you will soon experience some of the incredible benefits of walking this path. Your husband will feel respected and this respect can lead to love and relational intimacy – the very thing you crave.

Be ready and willing to genuinely apologize and to ask for forgiveness. Be a woman as rare as the rarest gem. Embrace the beauty, grace, and humility of a sincere apology and walk in the pleasing gaze of God.

Dear Lord,

When I need forgiveness from my husband, I don't enjoy asking for it. I would rather avoid the process altogether. It's so much easier to pass by the need to truly humble myself before my husband. But I want to grow and I want my husband and me to keep a spirit of openness and forgiveness in our marriage. The next time I wrong my husband, help me to be quick to reach out to him in humility, admit my guilt, and ask him to forgive me.

In Jesus' name, amen.

Ask your husband:

"Has there been a time recently when I wronged you or hurt you and should have asked you for forgiveness for something but didn't?" If he says yes, ask him to tell you what is on his mind and then take the opportunity to ask for his forgiveness right then. If he says no, tell him that you are really trying to grow in this.

Notes

Notes

27
A Strong-Hearted Woman

by Lisa

*The gentle, quiet spirit of the wise wife
moves with power and beauty.*

I'm not sure what started it.

But I suspect it had something to do with this one book I'd read a few years back. I'm not saying the author *intended* to communicate this message, but it's certainly what I concluded.

If I wanted to be a good wife – a biblical wife? Then I needed to tone it down a bit. A lot. I needed to swallow it, hold it back, and keep it down. I was far too intense for my own good. Or at least for my husband's own good.

So I started this new, radical campaign. I didn't even tell my husband what I was up to but decided that from then on, I was going to mellow out. Keep it quiet.

Now if you know me, you'll probably find that rather funny. You can hardly picture it.

But I really did try. And I kept it going fairly well . . . until one day when we were discussing a certain subject while standing by the piano – a subject that I felt somewhat *passionate* about. I couldn't take it any longer.

I nearly shouted, "I just can't *do* this!"

"Do what?" His eyebrows raised.

"I can't keep my mouth shut and not express all that I'm thinking or feeling!" I was practically shaking with frustration.

Then – being the sensitive soul that he is – he burst out laughing. I resisted the temptation of throwing the old red hymnal at him. But only barely.

I'm glad I didn't though because I might have missed what he said next. "But, babe, I don't want you to 'zip it.' I married you because I appreciate your strong mind and passionate heart. Don't you see? I *love* that about you."

Oh. You do?

At last, I was able to reconcile being a strong-hearted woman and being a biblical wife.

Now you might not see the struggle here. You're wondering, *What's the issue?*

Well, the "issue" is that the Bible talks about the "beauty of a gentle and quiet spirit" (1 Peter 3:4), and I truly wanted to fit that description. But I wasn't so sure that I did.

Maybe you're a strong-hearted woman, too. You don't give up, you're willing to stand up for what you believe is right, and you're passionate about your family and the world you live in.

I get that. And guess what? It's okay.

A strong-hearted woman can keep a quiet heart. She's not agitated in her spirit, yet remains strong in her convictions.

A strong-hearted woman readily respects her husband. She uses her strength to support her husband, not to go up against him.

A strong-hearted woman draws her strength from Christ, not from herself. God gave you that wonderful, passionate heart and, as long as you're submitted to Him, then you're right where He wants you to be.

Not only that, you're right where your husband wants you to be.

He loves you for it.

Dear Lord,

You know the way You made me. You know my passionate heart and my strong mind, and I thank You for those things. I pray that You'll help me to use my gifts, as well as to keep a gentle and quiet spirit.

In Jesus' name, amen.

Ask your husband:

"What are some things about my strong heart that you appreciate?" (You might have to explain to him what you mean by that.) "Do you see me as having a quiet spirit as well? Are there any areas in which you'd like me to express more . . . or maybe less?"

Notes

Notes

28

The Last Word

by Matthew

The wife who insists on having the last word soon discovers its value was grossly overrated.

We're good at keeping arguments going, aren't we? Not that we set out to "run a marathon," but we've managed to be at odds for hours . . . . Not good.

What are you communicating to your husband when you insist on having the last word in an argument?

Insisting on having the last word conveys to your husband that you are stubborn, willful, and care more about getting your way than you do about listening to what he has to say.

That's why, ultimately, he withdraws ... avoids ... pulls inward.

Not much of a win, is it?

Why do we put so high a value on having the last word? Because our enemy is very skilled at making the last word seem like a win. But really, how could it be a win if it results in your husband's silence and sullenness? What a powerful deception!

This impulse to "win" comes from somewhere ... somewhere not very good. The Bible makes it clear that contention comes from pride. (Proverbs 13:10)

Really? This is from pride?

Yes, really.

The next time you disagree on something and feel that rising impulse to answer back endlessly, it's time to pause. Yes, it's hard, and your spirit will fully resist you slowing down. But you can do it.

The next time you disagree on something, show him how much you respect him. Choose not to over-talk, out-debate, out-shout ... out-*anything*. In fact, you don't have to argue at all. Try calmly offering your perspective without needing to have an overly-intense response. Then graciously allow him to finish the conversation, even if you disagree with him.

If you practice calm conversations in which you show your husband this kind of respect, you will find that your quiet tone of voice will begin to carry more weight.

And that is a real win!

Dear Lord,

I do not want to be prideful, because I know You hate pride. The next time I feel the will to argue rising and the "need" to get the last word with my husband, help me to listen to Your voice and to check that destructive, aggressive spirit that strives to win. Lord, I want our marriage to win. Help me to focus on showing great respect to my husband the next time we have a disagreement.

In Jesus' name, amen.

ASK YOUR HUSBAND:

"When we have a disagreement, or when I have a difference of opinion and want to discuss it with you, what can I do or change in my approach or manner that will make it easier for you to hear me?"

Notes

29

The Power of Prayer

by Lisa

*The yielded spirit of the praying wife
has the power of Heaven behind her.*

He wasn't about to budge.

That much was evident. I could see it in his eyes, tell by his body language. My husband was in his "brick wall mode" and he wasn't moving.

All I'd done was to ask him to change – only change this *one thing* that was bothering me – and yet he was rather closed to the idea. Completely closed, in fact. I'm not even sure he was listening.

What to do now?

That's what I was left wondering. Because I sure wanted

him to do it differently.

I figured I had options. I might resort to crying, yelling, whining, pouting or maybe some serious nagging – although I'd have to admit I've never had much success with any of those approaches. Nor could I find any support for those methods in the Bible.

No, I would have to come up with a better plan. So, with a big, heavy sigh, I began praying.

Not a stiff, formal prayer, but a pour-your-heart-out and a *Lord-You-made-this-man-so-now-what?* kind of prayer.

And then I waited. Prayed some more. Waited and waited and waited.

Still nothing.

Then I did what came naturally – *I gave up.* And our life continued on as usual.

Until one day while I was chopping vegetables in the kitchen, he walked by me and dropped a simple remark. It went something like this, "You know that thing that was bugging you? Well, I've decided I'm not going to do it anymore." And that was that.

Can you believe it? That brick wall of mine had moved after all.

I didn't say much but continued dicing the onions. With tears streaming down my cheeks. *(Silly onions, what they'll do to a woman.)*

God had changed what I could not. He had answered my prayers, and He'd been working all along. I just couldn't see it.

And that might be where you're at right now. You're in that place of waiting and praying and more waiting. Maybe it's over something quite big, or maybe only a tiny matter. But either way, it's a blessing and a comfort to bring it all before the Lord and know that He's listening. *He's always listening.*

So the most powerful move you can make in your marriage?

Pray.

Pray for him. Pray for you. Ask God to do His mighty work in your marriage. Thank Him for what He's already doing – where you can see it and even where you can't just yet.

Because if He can move mountains? Then He can move brick walls.

I know. I've watched Him move mine.

Dear Lord,

Help me to trust You to change what I cannot. I have faith that since You are able to move mountains, You can move my husband, too. Please work in His life, as I know You're working in mine.

In Jesus' name, amen.

CHALLENGE:

Commit that you will not say anything to your husband, but go to God in prayer with the issue that's been weighing on your heart. Patiently petition the Lord each day and wait to see how He answers your prayers.

Notes

Notes

30
Passionate Love
by Matthew

Warm hugs, sincere kisses, and frequent lovemaking make the tempter's job much harder.

In our sex-saturated society, no one needs to be told that there is temptation everywhere for everyone. When it comes to playing dirty with sexuality, Satan is having a heyday. It can be dangerous to walk outside your door, go to the mall, or click on the internet.

But God has a lot to say about the topic of sex, too.

Many are surprised to learn that the Bible encourages couples to have sex regularly. But this is for a very practical reason.

Why?

Paul tells believers, "Don't withhold sex from one another except by mutual agreement and only for a specific time, that you might give yourselves to fasting and prayer; and then commence having regular sex, that Satan not tempt you." (1 Corinthians 7:5, my paraphrase)

As a woman, you desire that your man pursue you and cherish you. You want him to initiate romance and love being with you. There are a lot of men who need to improve in this area but don't allow his need for improvement to prevent you from the powerful role you play.

Don't underestimate or neglect the allure of your interested womanly heart.

Accept your husband's advances. Frequent loving hugs, warm kisses, kind words, and overt sexual interest make the tempter's job in your marriage much more difficult.

Dear Lord,

I want there to be a wall of love around my husband and me that makes each of us strong in a sea of temptation. Help me to focus less on the quality of his advances and more on the quality of my response. Help me to focus less on the quantity of his need and more on the quantity of my initiation.

In Jesus' name, amen.

ASK YOUR HUSBAND:

"Are you happy with how often we have sex? Is there a time of day or night that you especially enjoy being intimate? How can I better fulfill your sexual needs?"

Notes

31
No Tomorrow

by Lisa

Love your husband like there's no tomorrow,
because tomorrow may never come.

*G*uess what happened early last Sunday morning to my pastor husband?

My beloved slipped on the ice in our front yard and cracked his head.

How he managed to walk back into the house, I don't know. But I took one look at him and could tell that something was wrong. Very wrong.

"What happened to you?"

"I fell. Not sure I'm going to be able to preach today."

And then he turned around and I saw the back of his head. And that awful smashed spot.

Nope. No preaching that day.

And then, being the caring, compassionate wife that I am, I found myself suddenly becoming . . . mad.

I was mad that he got hurt. Mad that he hadn't been more careful. Mad that we were going to miss church. Just plain mad.

If this sounds like a strange response to you, then I'd have to agree. It is an odd response.

Thankfully, I didn't say anything or let him know how I was feeling. I just sort of stared at him (Okay, honestly, if he ever "just sort of stared at me" if I came in the house with a cracked head? There'd be big trouble. Big, *big* trouble.).

But then I saw that he looked as though he was getting woozy as if he was going to pass out or something. That snapped me out of it.

"Go lay down!"

So our older daughter took the rest of the children to church and left him and me alone on a Sunday morning. Just the two of us. And I watched over him while he rested.

And I thought about all the things I hadn't yet said to him. I even tried to imagine what my life would be like without him, but I couldn't do it.

A few hours later, when he felt more like talking, I told him what was on my mind. I told him how grateful I was to have the chance to say the words that I'd been meaning to say, more time to love him better.

He laughed.

Not seeing the humor, I asked him what that was supposed to be mean? (And you thought my earlier response was strange!)

He told me that while he was laying there on the ice, all he could think about were all the things he'd not yet done for me. And it made him sad to think he might not have the chance.

I guess that *is* kind of funny. In a lovey-dovey sort of way.

Ever since that near-tragic morning, you might have noticed some small things, if you'd been around us much. How we reach for one another more often than ever. How we hold each other even closer. More whisperings and more lighthearted laughter.

The kind of things that come about when you've had a close call.

And that experience makes me want to reach out to you, too. To urge you to consider whether you've said all the loving things you've meant to say, or have done all the loving things you've wanted to do. If not . . .

Say them and do them now. *Today.*

Say the words. Write the note. Pick up the phone. Do the things.

No need to wait for a close call. We only have today. Make the most of the time you've been given.

Dear Lord,

I don't want to take today for granted, treating my husband as if how I interact with him isn't all that important because "there is always tomorrow." Help me to love him well today, because "today" is all You've given to us. Time with my husband is a precious gift. Help me not to waste that time, starting right now.

In Jesus' name, amen.

Ask your husband:

"What if one of us were to find out that we only had a few more months to live? What do you think would change in our marriage?"

Notes

Notes

Conclusion

*H*ere we are at the end of thirty-one chapters and we've talked through rather personal and challenging aspects of marriage together. Some inspiring, some insightful, and some a little convicting, too. But our hope is that you come away feeling encouraged and better equipped than ever to be the kind of wife you've always wanted to be after reading this devotional.

Please know that Matthew and I have poured our hearts into these pages and that we've prayed – and continue to pray – for every wife who reads our words here. You might be a newlywed or you might have been married for decades. No matter what your situation or where you're at with your husband, we believe our God is a Redeemer and He is more than able to do His work in you and in your marriage. He is with you and you are not alone.

So now walk in wisdom and grow in love.

And watch how God changes your marriage along the way.

MATT AND LISA

Dear Lord,

We thank You for each wife who is reading the pages here. We ask that You fill her heart with Your love and a deep sense of Your work in her life. Where she is discouraged, we pray You give her hope. Where she is convicted, we pray You give her strength to do what's right. Where she is worried or anxious, we pray You give her peace. Help her to walk in wisdom, practice kindness, and enjoy a beautiful, loving marriage that honors You.

In Jesus' name, amen.

I want to encourage you to visit **Club31Women.com**, a special gathering place to find inspiration and practical help in our relationships as wife, mother, homemaker, friend, and neighbor.

facebook.com/Club31Women

instagram.com/club31women

pinterest.com/Club31Women

twitter.com/LisaClub31Women

Club31Women

I'd like to invite you to join me at **MatthewLJacobson.com** where we discuss marriage, parenting, Church, and culture.

facebook.com/matthewljacobson

instagram.com/matthewljacobson

pinterest.com/MatthewLJ

twitter.com/MLJacobson

Matthew Jacobson

Also available from Lisa Jacobson:

LISA JACOBSON

LIKE YOU,
WE'RE ON A
LIFE-LONG JOURNEY
OF LEARNING TO
LOVE EACH OTHER.

100 WAYS TO
LOVE
YOUR HUSBAND

God wants your marriage to be beautiful and resilient.
This book offers specific, real-life instruction on how
to enjoy the best marriage has to offer.

www.LoyalArtsMedia.com

Also available from Matthew L. Jacobson:

LIKE YOU,
WE'RE ON A
LIFE-LONG JOURNEY
OF LEARNING TO
LOVE EACH OTHER.

100 WAYS TO
LOVE
YOUR WIFE

MATTHEW L. JACOBSON

Practical, hands-on advice you can start applying immediately - for the soon-to-be married man, as well as the "veteran" husband.

The companion to *Marriage Wisdom for Her*

MATTHEW L. JACOBSON

Marriage Wisdom

FOR HIM

A 31 DAY DEVOTIONAL
FOR BUILDING A BETTER MARRIAGE

www.LoyalArtsMedia.com